Y0-AKM-860

DISCARDED

Let's Go on a Space Shuttle

TIME: fifteen years from now
PLACE: a space shuttle
MISSION: to carry an observatory into outer space
PURPOSE OF MISSION: to collect scientific information
about the stars

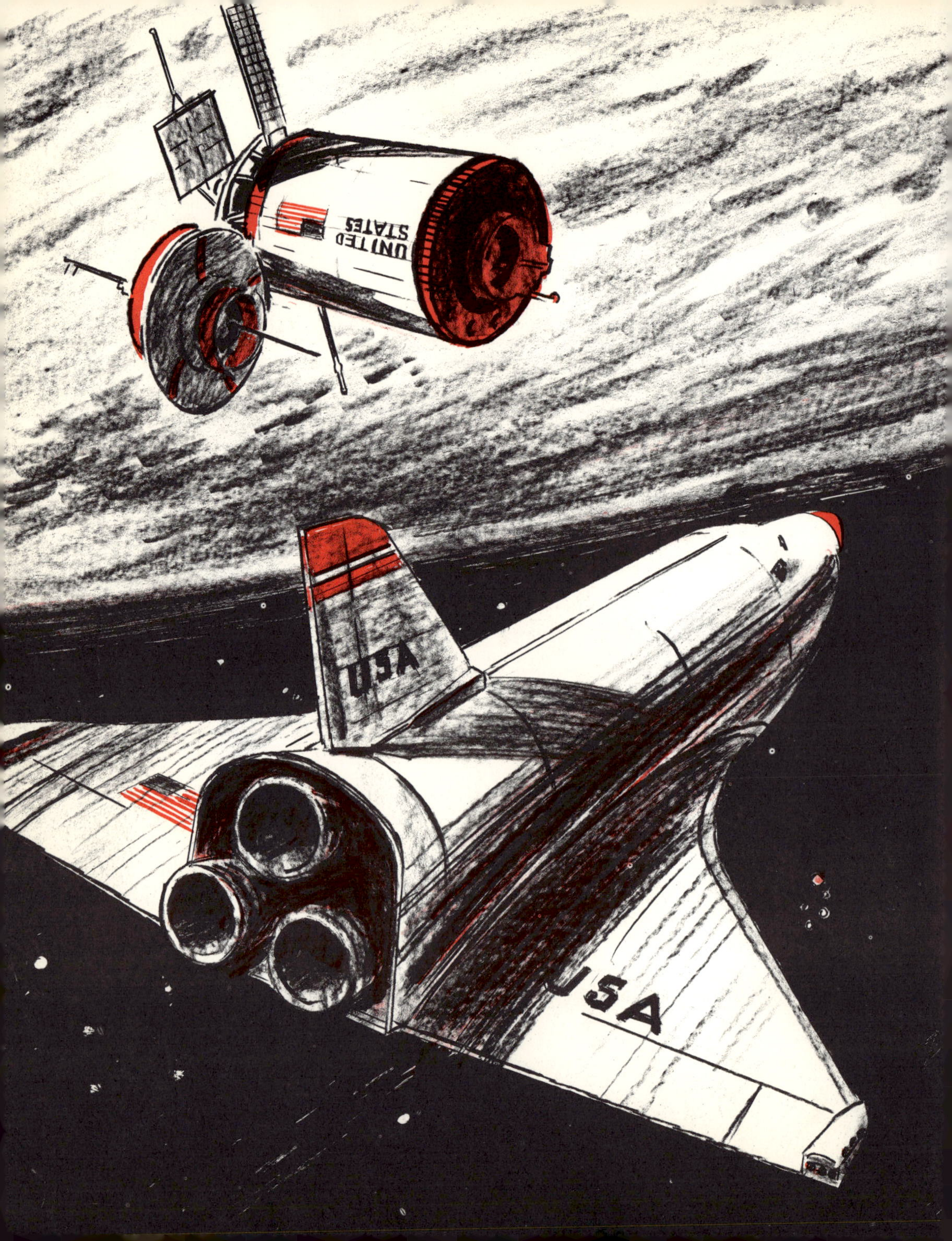
USA
USA

Let's Go on a
SPACE
SHUTTLE

by Michael Chester

illustrated by
Albert Micale

G. P. PUTNAM'S SONS   NEW YORK

Text Copyright © 1975 by Michael Chester
Illustrations Copyright © 1975 by Albert Micale
All rights reserved. Published simultaneously in
Canada by Longman Canada Limited, Toronto.
SBN:GB-399-60960-1
SBN:TR-399-20470-9
Library of Congress Catalog Card Number:
PRINTED IN THE UNITED STATES OF AMERICA

The time is fifteen years in the future, and you are an astronaut. You are a member of a ship's crew. The ship is called a "Space Shuttle," and it is much more advanced than the spaceships of the past.

The spaceship is made up of several different sections, or *modules*. The part of the ship where you and three other astronauts ride is called the *orbiter*. It is like a large airplane with stubby wings and a tail structure. The orbiter is mounted piggyback on a huge fuel tank —bigger than the orbiter itself. Two powerful solid-fuel booster rockets are also mounted on the side of the tank.

Most spaceships are completely used up in a single mission. Most of a spaceship's stages are jettisoned into space when they have burned all their fuel. But the Space Shuttle is not like that. Except for the fuel tank, the entire ship is brought back from space and used again in other missions. This makes it a very practical and useful kind of spaceship. It also makes the cost of space missions much lower.

The blast-off from the launch pad is much like that of earlier spaceships such as the Apollo moonship, except that the rocket blast is "softer." You and the other three astronauts are belted into your contour seats in the crew quarters at the nose end of the orbiter. As the three rockets at the tail end of the orbiter and the two big booster rockets all begin to blast, the whole ship shudders and starts to rise.

You feel the force of the rocket blast pressing you against the back of your seat. But the pressure does not feel as great as it did for earlier astronauts. The Space Shuttle gives its crew a much smoother ride into space.

You are used to this ride into space, because you have already made several missions on board this spaceship. Your last mission was completed only two weeks ago. There has been plenty of time for you to rest, and plenty of time for flight mechanics to get the Shuttle ready. You know, too, that you will be going on another mission after you have finished this one. You and the other astronauts on board the ship are the regular crew, and you expect to make many flights on this same ship.

A few minutes after blast-off, you feel a jolt as the two booster rockets are jettisoned. They have done their job, boosting you out of the atmosphere with their great power. Parachutes will open to slow the fall of the boosters through the air. They will drift downward until they splash into the ocean. Ships will pick up these booster rockets, and later they will be packed with a new supply of solid rocket fuel and made ready for another mission.

The three rockets at the tail end of your orbiter continue to blast. They burn liquid rocket fuel and, as fast as that fuel is burned, more is pumped into the engines from the big tank. Several minutes after blast-off, the tank is empty. You feel another jolt as the tank is jettisoned into space. But a full supply of fuel is now left in the orbiter's rockets, and the rockets continue to blast. When they stop blasting, you are in orbit in outer space.

As in any orbiting spaceship, there is no feeling of "up" and "down" for the crew members. You and the other astronauts are able to float easily from place to place inside the ship, holding on to guidelines to pull yourself along.

There are three decks in the crew quarters. The first deck is where all the ship's

FLIGHT SECTION

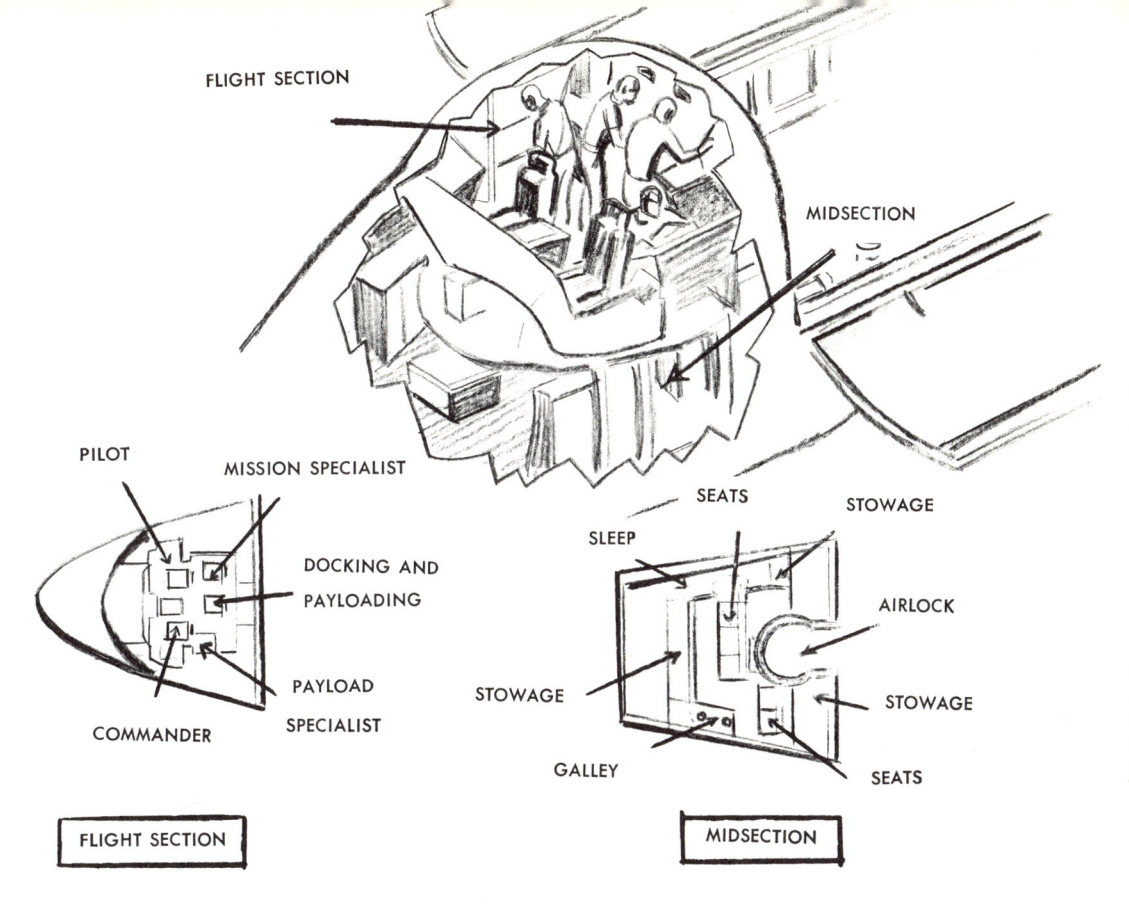

MIDSECTION

PILOT
MISSION SPECIALIST
DOCKING AND PAYLOADING
PAYLOAD SPECIALIST
COMMANDER

FLIGHT SECTION

SEATS
STOWAGE
SLEEP
AIRLOCK
STOWAGE
STOWAGE
GALLEY
SEATS

MIDSECTION

controls are located. On the second deck are the ship's living quarters, where there are bunks, tables, a bathroom, and food supplies for you and the other members of the crew. The third deck contains electronic equipment and wiring. Crew members visit that deck only to inspect or repair the equipment.

13

In this early part of the mission, all four of you are on the first deck, busy at your jobs. The commander and the copilot are operating the ship's controls and talking with people at the Mission Control Center on the ground in order to report on the flight and to get instructions.

The third astronaut, the *mission specialist,* is sitting at a table, studying charts. His job is to keep careful track of this particular mission and to see that all the mission goals are completed. The purpose of the mission is to carry a special satellite into orbit. This satellite is an *orbital observatory.* It has telescopes, radio antennas, its own computer, and other instruments. When it is left in orbit around the earth, it will radio scientific data about the stars back to tracking stations on the ground.

You are the *payload specialist* on board the Space Shuttle. The *payload* is whatever the ship is carrying in its big *cargo bay*. On this mission, the payload is the orbital observatory. On other missions, other kinds of satellites and scientific units are carried into space by the Shuttle.

You are well prepared for this work. You have studied science in college and you have been through special training as a test pilot and as a flight engineer. You are very familiar with the problems of air and space flight. In an emergency situation, you would be able to take over the job of piloting the ship. In fact, every member of the crew knows something about all of the jobs that are to be carried out, and each is able to substitute for the others.

You go to a window at the rear of the first deck and look back into the cargo bay. The cargo bay is a very large section of the orbiter. It stretches 18 meters (60 feet) in length. The cargo bay is lit with floodlights, so you can see the big satellite there. There is a control panel near the window, and you push buttons to test some of the electronic units on the satellite. You have to make sure that the satellite is in good operating condition before you eject it into space. Taking care of the payload and watching over everything that happens in the cargo room is your special job on board the Space Shuttle.

Most of the tests that you carry out show that the satellite equipment is in perfect condition. But a red light flashes on your panel, telling you that a battery-charging unit needs to be replaced. You will have to go into the cargo bay to do that repair job.

Before going into the cargo bay, you report the problem to the commander. Then you get into your space suit. You have to wear a space suit to enter the cargo bay because there is no air there. It can be filled with air if there is a special reason to fill it. But on this mission there was no such reason, so it is not a place where a person can go without wearing a space suit. The space suit protects you in many ways. It keeps you warm, it protects you from the very low-pressure conditions of the airless cargo bay, and it has a built-in air supply for you to breathe.

To go into the cargo bay, you have to pull yourself, half crawling and half floating, through a tunnel-shaped *airlock*. This passageway leads from the second deck back to the cargo bay. After you enter the airlock, you close the airtight door to the crew quarters to keep the air from escaping into the cargo bay. Then you enter the cargo bay, closing a second airtight door behind you. Only a small amount of air escapes into the cargo bay.

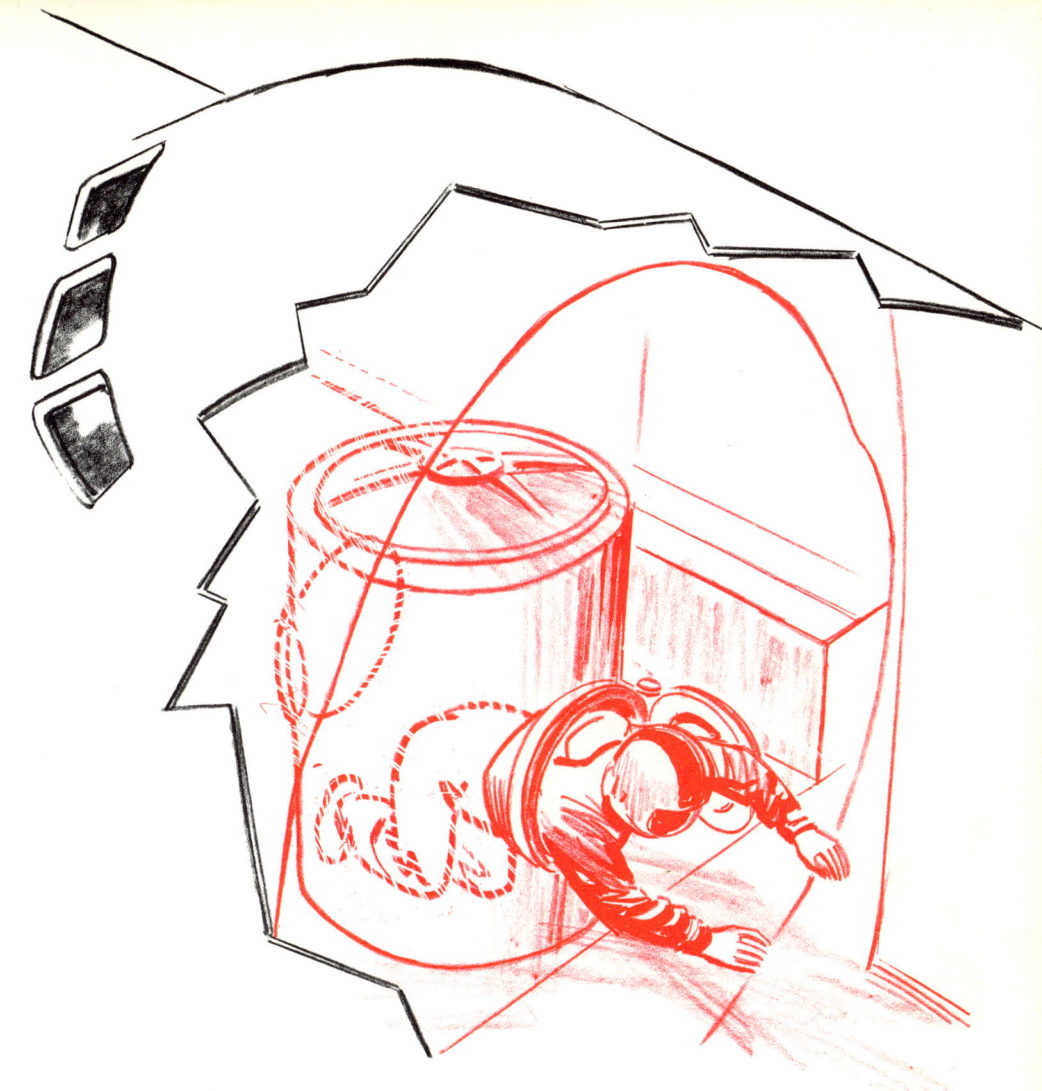

19

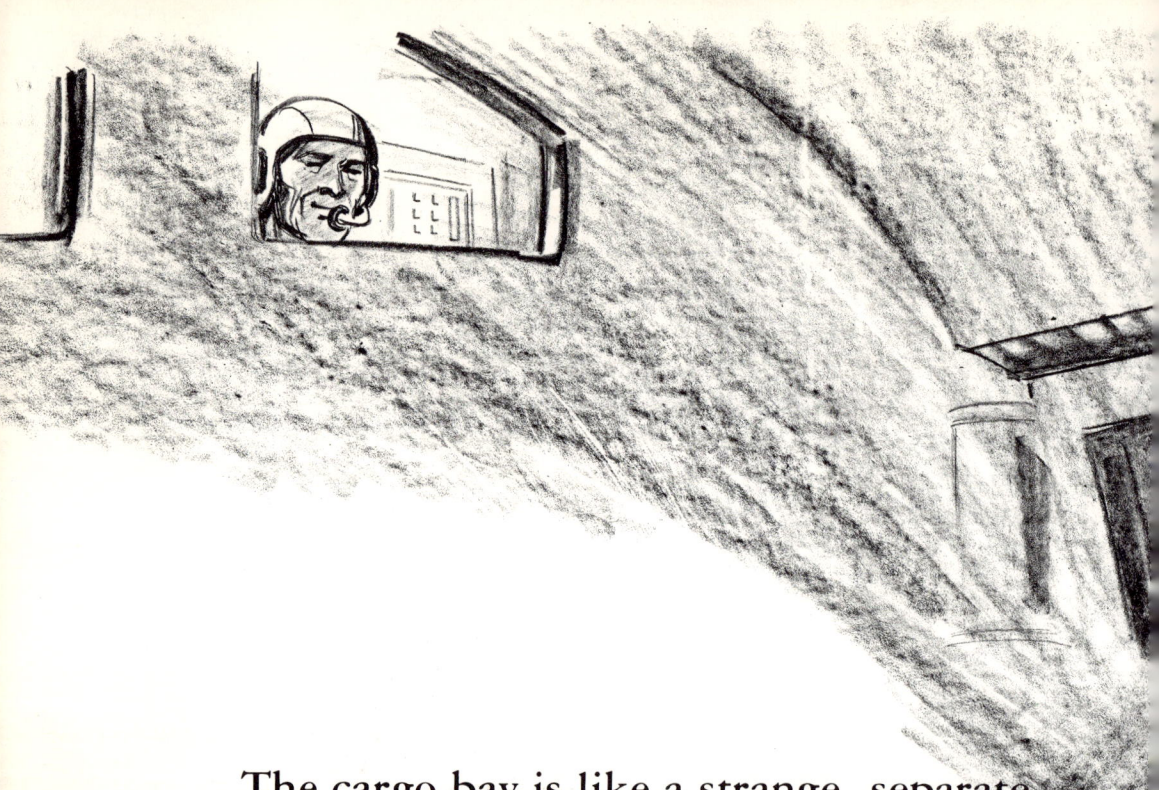

The cargo bay is like a strange, separate world, apart from the rest of the ship. But you are not really alone here. One of the other astronauts is watching you through the same window where you yourself were looking into the cargo bay a short time ago. A radio set in the helmet of your space suit allows you to talk with him and to let him know how the repair job is going.

The repairs do not take very long. You remove the battery-charging unit from the satellite and put a new unit in its place. Then you return through the airlock, closing the doors at each end of the lock behind you.

You have brought the faulty unit back with you. After you have climbed out of your space suit, you study it to see what went wrong. It is important to find out what the trouble was because if you understand what is causing it, you may be able to prevent its happening again.

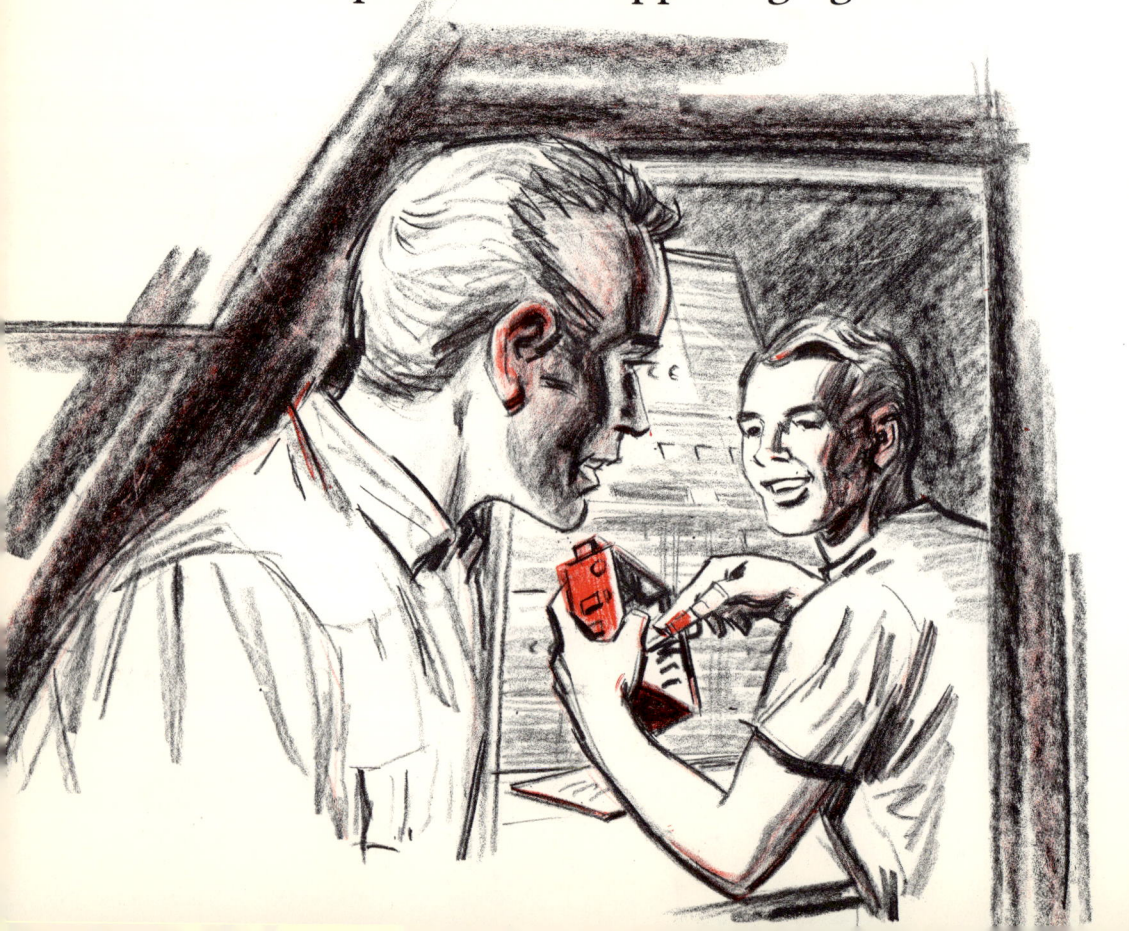

These first few hours are only the beginning of the mission. After this, many days pass, as the details of the mission are carried out. At a number of different times, the ship's rockets are ignited again to correct the orbit. While the rockets blast, the weightless condition inside the ship ends for a short time, as the force of the rocket blast makes one end of the ship feel like a floor. Then the blast stops, and you are weightless again.

Finally, the time comes to launch the payload satellite into space, where it can begin its work as an orbital observatory. You are in charge of that launching. You sit at the panel at the rear of the crew quarters and look through the window while you operate remote controls.

Using these controls, you open up a whole section of the covered hull of the cargo bay. As the section of hull swings outward, you can see the black sky of outer space and the bright, steadily shining stars. You set a big mechanical arm into motion inside the cargo bay. It lifts the satellite out of the ship, and holds it there.

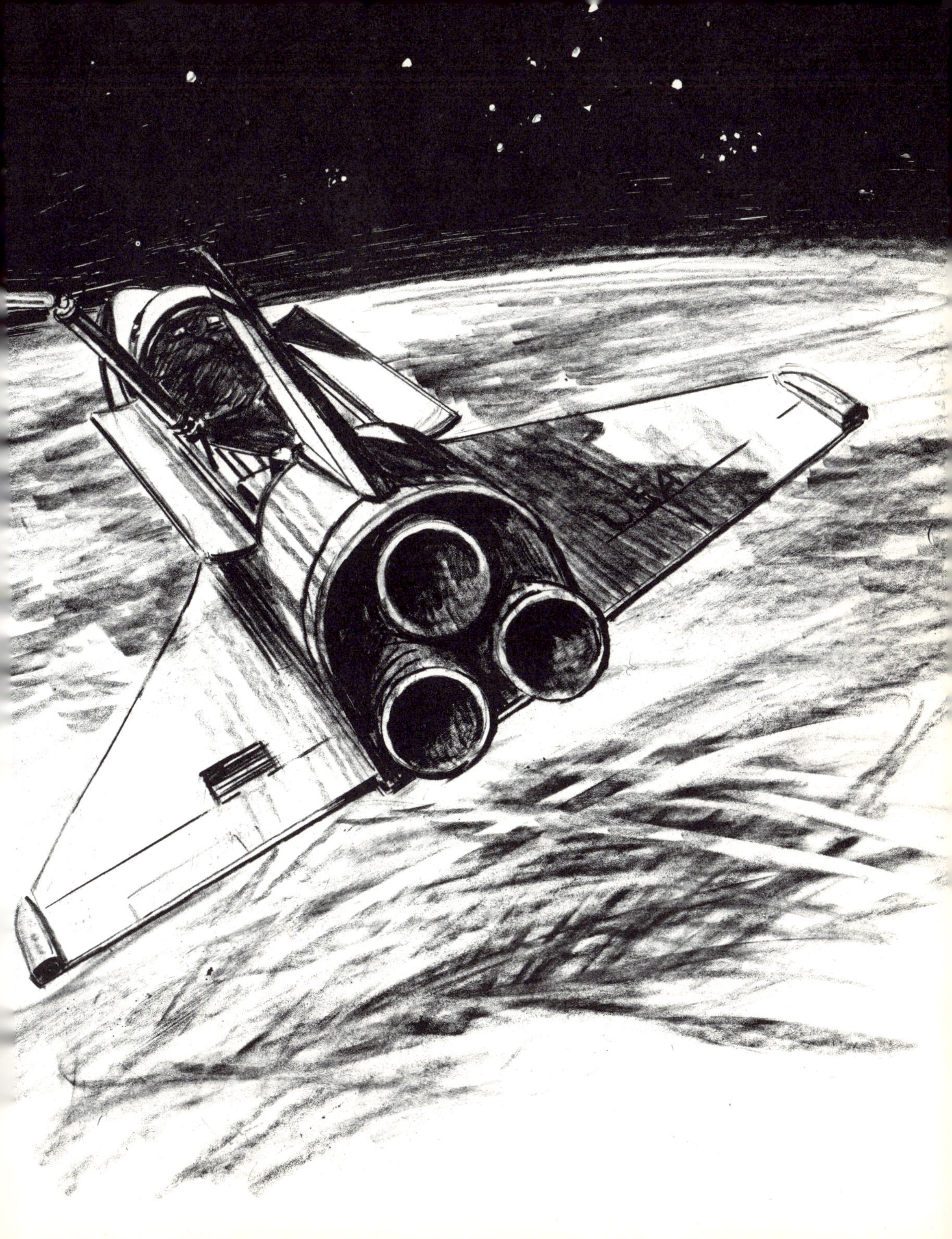
USA

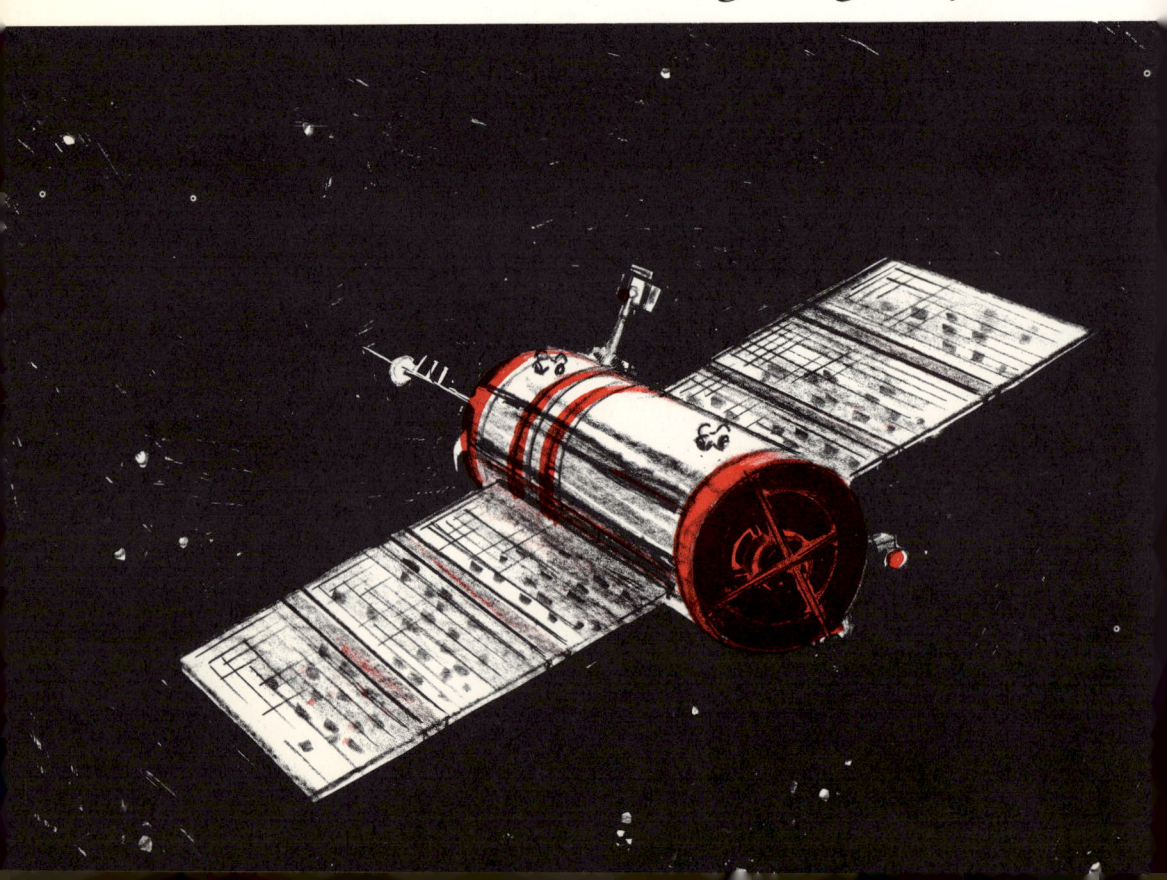

There are still electrical cables connecting the satellite to the orbiter, so you are still able to check out systems on board the satellite, using the switches and dials on your control panel. When you find that everything is working as it should, you make the steel arm release the satellite. The satellite is now orbiting alongside your ship. The electrical cables also are snapped loose from the satellite and reeled back into the cargo bay. You press the button that closes the cargo bay.

You are still able to send radio signals to the satellite, so you can still test units on board it and send correction signals if necessary. In case of real difficulty, you can even cross over to the satellite, using a safety line and a small cold-gas propulsion unit with a miniature rocket nozzle.

When you are satisfied that the satellite is operating perfectly, you radio a message back to Mission Control saying that all is well. But your ship stays in orbit alongside the satellite for many more hours in order to monitor its operation. One time the ship begins to drift a little too close to the satellite, and the copilot has to fire a small control rocket to ease the ship away, avoiding a collision.

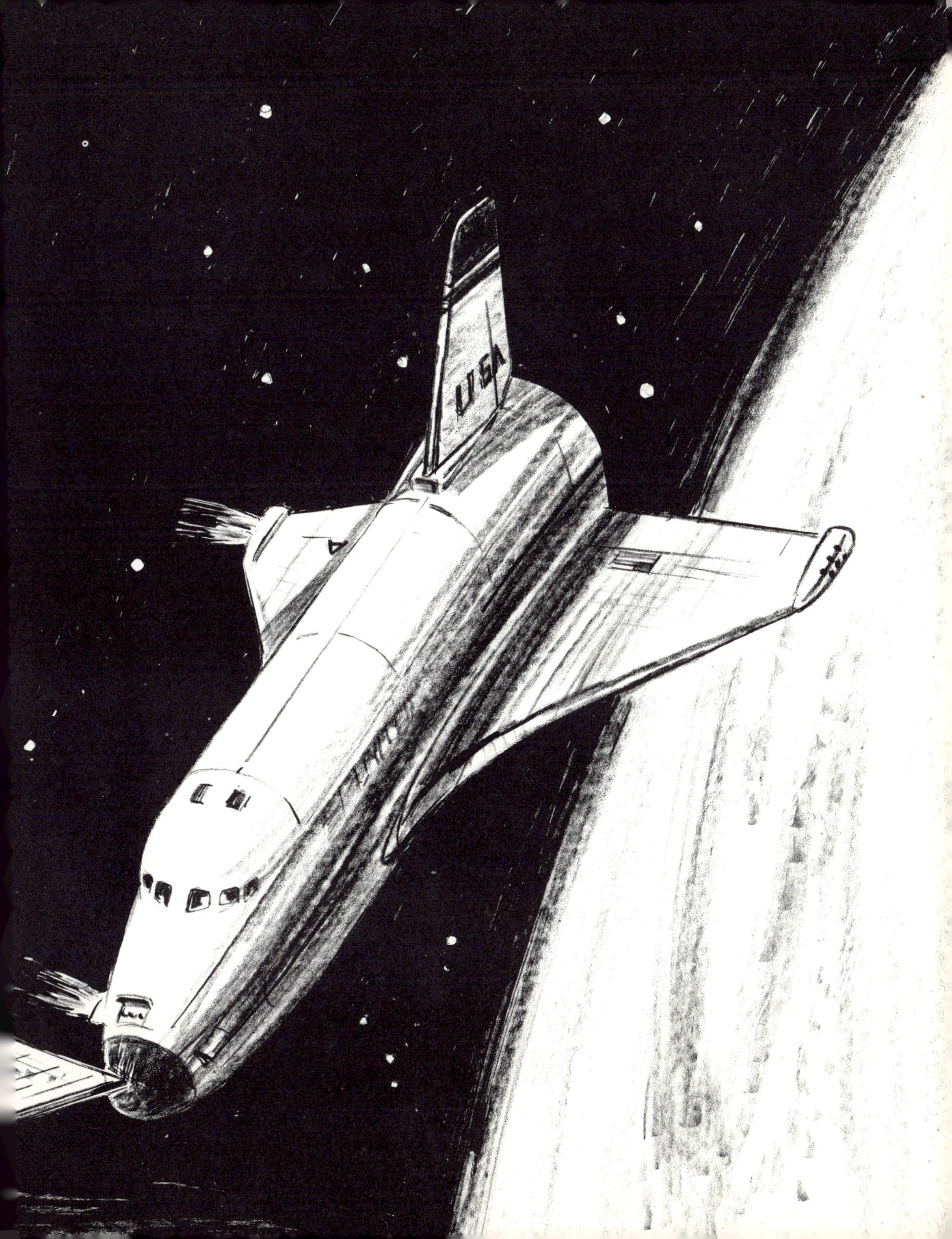

You look out through a porthole at the satellite. It looks strange and eerie, moving in its lonely orbit through space. Its big panels of solar cells are spread out like wings. These solar cells collect sunlight and convert it into electricity, so that the satellite's batteries can be recharged. You also see the radio antennas on the satellite. It turns very slowly (too slowly to see), so that its signals, reporting scientific information, are beamed back to earth.

You realize that you may see this satellite again, perhaps many years from now. Many of your missions will involve repairing satellites that are already in orbit. On some missions, satellites may be collected from orbit and transported back to earth by the Shuttle. At some future time, you may be visiting the orbital observatory to repair or collect it.

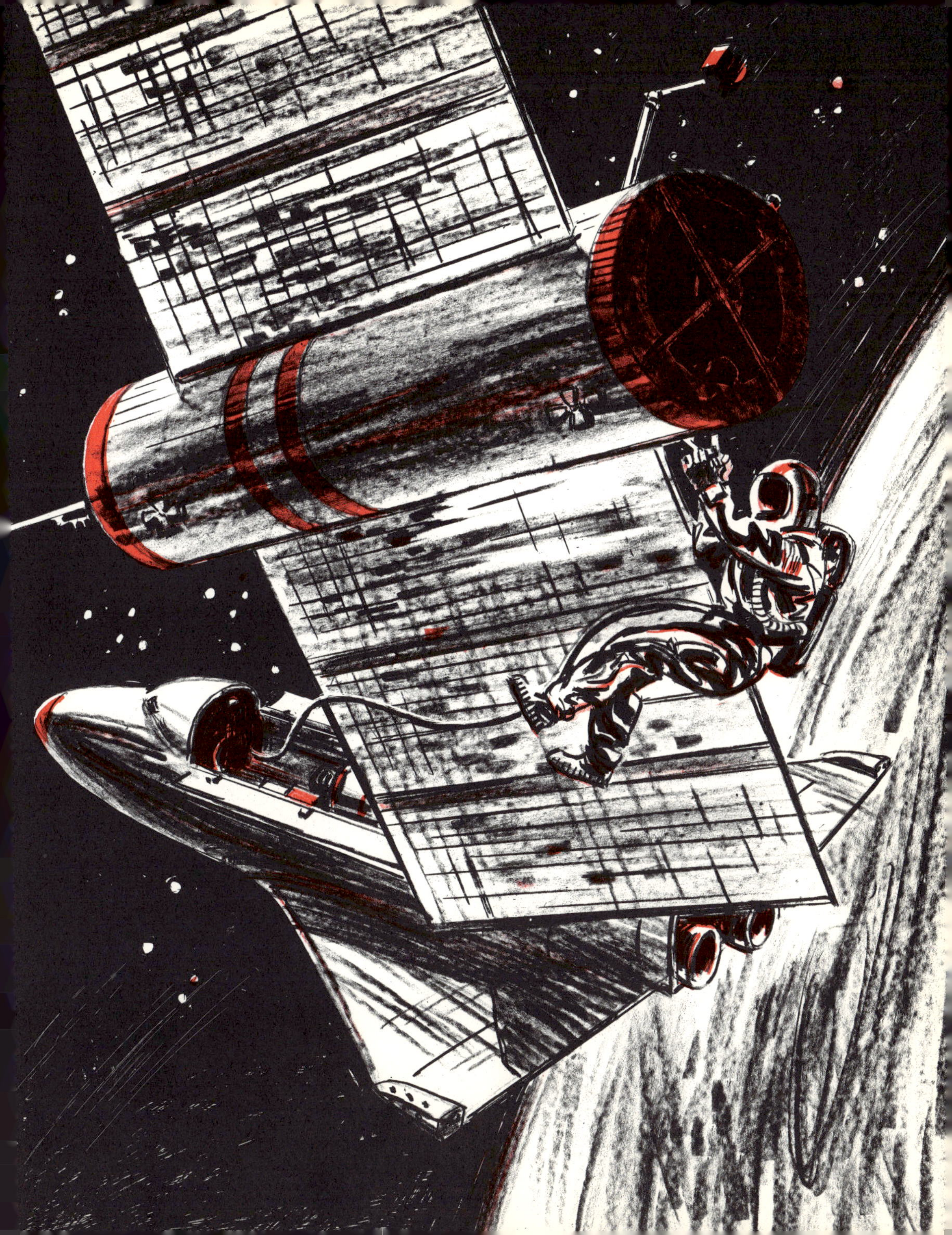

After the orbital observatory has been completely checked in orbit, it is time for your ship to return to earth. The orbiter's retrorockets blast, slowing the ship down, so that it noses downward toward the earth. As the orbiter starts to reenter the atmosphere, you and the other members of the crew belt yourselves into your seats.

This part of the journey is rough. The force of the reentry makes the orbiter shudder and shake. In spite of the tremendous heat caused by the reentry, special heat-resistant materials on the hull keep the ship from becoming too hot.

At lower altitudes in the air, the airplane shape of the orbiter at last becomes comes useful. Turboprop engines roar into operation, and the commander and copilot fly the orbiter toward an airfield. The motion of the ship becomes smoother. Now, as in an airliner, there is an up-and-down of a more "usual" kind. The first deck, where the controls are located, is now an upper deck. This ship, which was a rocketing spaceship while it was in outer space, is now a jet aircraft. It comes in for a landing.

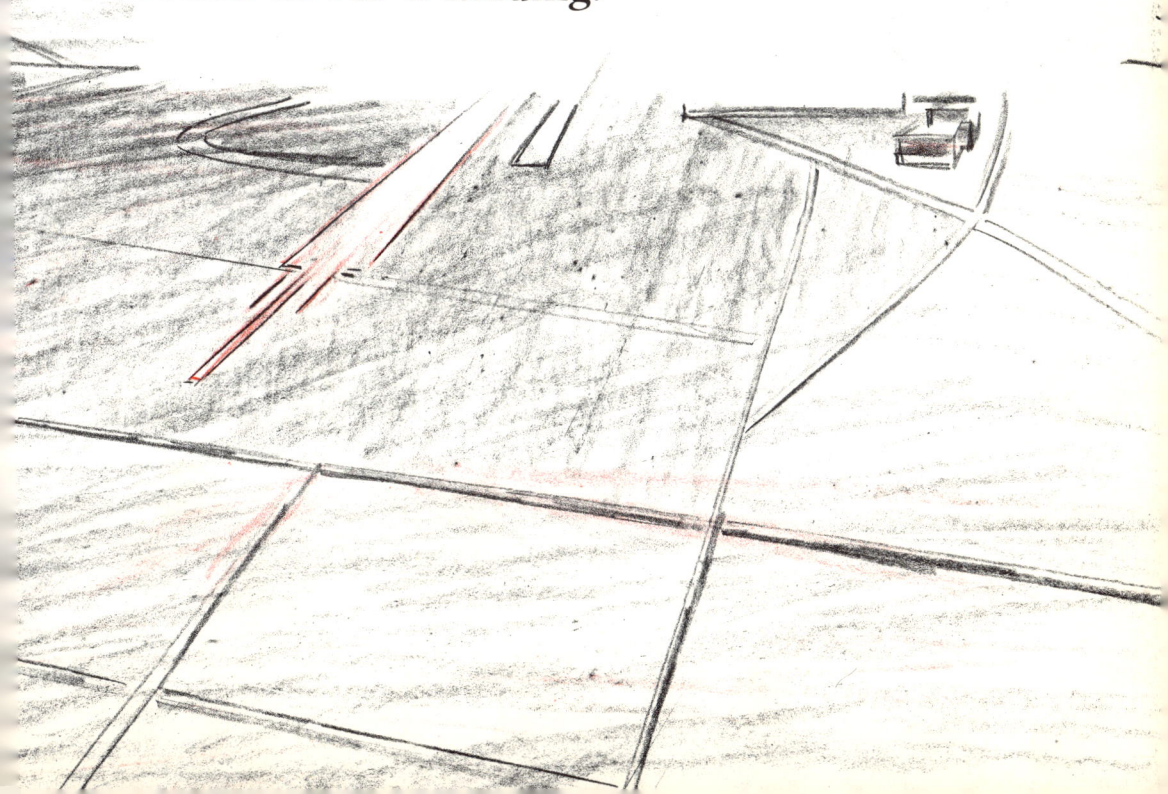

You and the orbiter have come home. Soon ground crews will be getting it ready for its next flight. Again, it is time for you to rest, and also to carry out some job assignments on the ground. In a month, it will be time to go into space again. Even while you are relaxing, you are starting to think about the next mission.

Thirty days later, the time comes for that next mission. You are back on board the spaceship. As usual, your job is to take care of the payload. On this mission, the payload is an entire space lab, manned by six scientists. The space lab is so big that it fills the entire cargo bay of the orbiter. The scientists are on board the space lab. You and the other three astronauts are in your crew quarters.

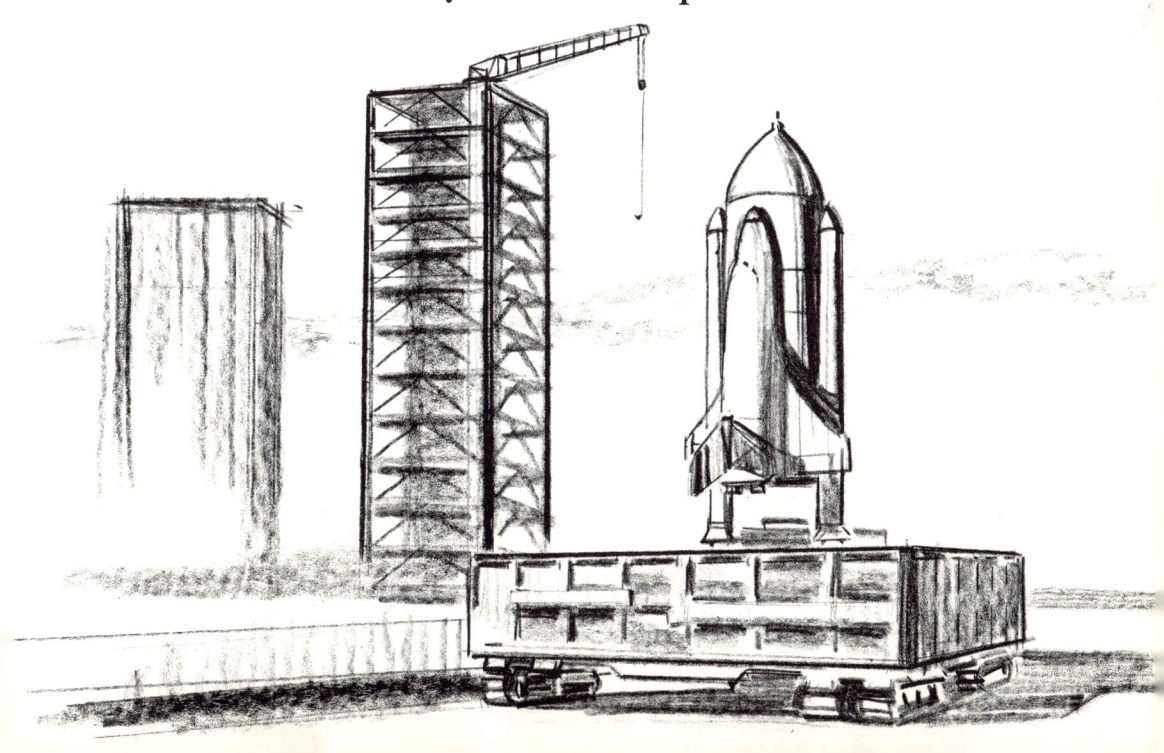

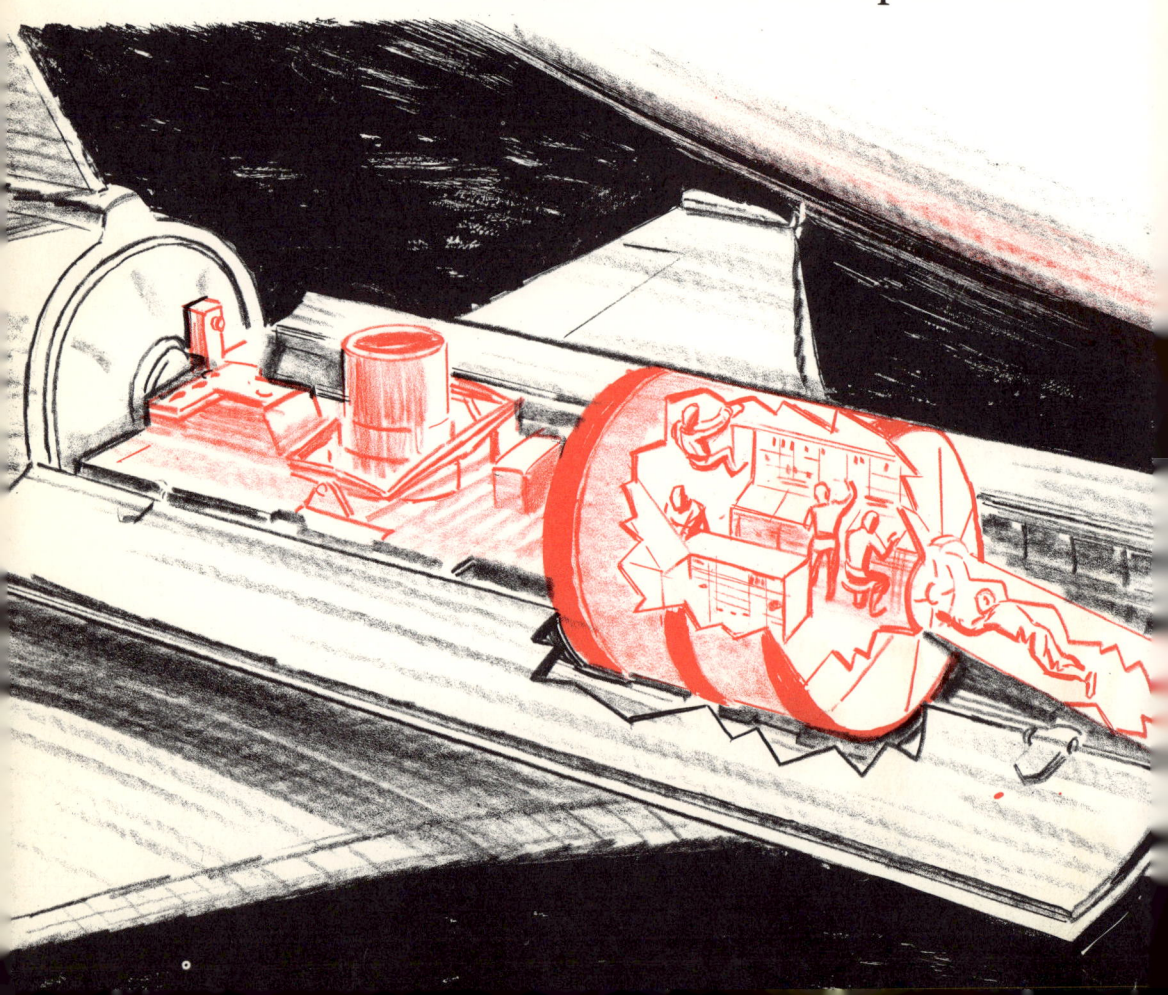

At first, this mission is like the last one, as the Shuttle blasts into orbit. But the rest of the mission is different from before. To begin with, the space lab will not be released into space. It will stay inside the orbiter. Scientists inside the space lab will carry out experiments especially designed for outer space. Some of these experiments may depend mainly on the weightless condition of the orbiting spaceship. Others may have to do with the measurement of radiation in outer space. And there are many other valuable experiments possible on board an orbiting spaceship that could not be done on earth.

On this mission, the airlock from the crew quarters is attached to the airlock of the space lab, so that it is possible to go back and forth directly between the two areas. As the payload specialist, you make many trips to help maintain instruments and electronic controls in the space lab. The scientists in the space lab also use the connecting tunnel often, as they come to the forward end of the ship to spend time in the crew quarters.

This voyage is a long one. The ship orbits through space for a month. You spend your time during that month in different parts of the ship—sometimes on the decks of the crew quarters, and sometimes in the space lab. Sometimes, too, you wear your space suit and go outside the ship to work on units located on the outer hull. Moving along on the outside of the hull, with another astronaut, you see the enormous blazing universe of stars stretching everywhere, and even this great ship seems suddenly small. Back inside the crew quarters, you relax, talking with some of the off-duty scientists.

The scientists ask you about some of the other missions that you have made on the Space Shuttle. You tell them about your last mission with the orbital observatory. You also tell them about a mission that was very important for you, in which you and your crewmates on the Shuttle rescued the crew of another spaceship that was damaged. In the early years of

RESCUE ORBITER

DISABLED ORBITER

MANIPULATOR ARM

space travel, there would have been no way to rescue the trapped crew. But the shuttle was able to pull alongside the damaged ship. All the trapped astronauts were rescued and brought back to earth.

After your active hours of work and relaxation, you lie in your bunk as the ship carries you through space. Before you fall asleep, you think of many things—especially of people whom you want to see when you get home. But, once in a while, you think of your next mission, to be made in a few months. The Shuttle will carry a robot spaceship into orbit and launch it on a trip toward the planet Saturn, where it will carry out a detailed investigation of Saturn's rings, in search of new scientific knowledge.

You know that many adventurous missions of different kinds lie ahead of you. These missions are possible because, after the early years of the space age, a ship was finally designed that could go back and forth on repeated missions—a ship able to carry out exact maneuvers in space. Part spaceship and part airplane, the Space Shuttle has made space flight a practical kind of operation. With its stubby wings, its big cargo bay, its mechanical arm, and its strange piggyback way of climbing into space, it is a ship that can do many things.

GLOSSARY

Airlock — a passageway to outer space or to any airless section of the ship, that an astronaut can go through without letting much air escape from the ship's cabin. (p. 18)

Cargo bay — the large section of the orbiter where the payload is carried. (p. 15)

Cold-gas propulsion unit — a small tank of cold high-pressure gas (such as carbon dioxide) that an astronaut can squirt to give himself a small boost through space. (p. 28)

Commander — the astronaut who is in charge of the spaceship, acting also as chief pilot. (p. 14)

Copilot — the astronaut who acts as assistant pilot. (p. 14)

Jettison — to drop a module of a spaceship—either to be left in space or to be recovered in the sea. (p. 6)

Mission specialist — the astronaut who is specially trained in the details of the particular mission. (p. 14)

Modules — separate sections of a spaceships. (p. 5)
Orbital observatory — a satellite with telescopes to observe the stars and report findings back to earth by radio. (p. 14)
Orbiter — the airplanelike module of the Space Shuttle that carries the astronauts in orbit and later flies to earth for a landing. (p. 5)
Payload — the satellite or space lab or whatever other object is being carried into space. (p. 15)
Payload specialist — the astronaut who is specially trained in checking the payload and ejecting it into orbit. (p. 15)
Retrorocket — a rocket engine that blasts in a forward direction to slow a spaceship to a lower speed. (p. 32)
Satellite — any object that orbits in space around the earth. (p. 14)
Solar cells — plates of solid material that collect sunlight and change it into electrical power. (p. 30)
Space lab — a scientific laboratory that is carried into space. (p. 38)

Other Things to Do While Reading
Let's Go on a Space Shuttle
1. How is a space shuttle like a bus? Like a moving van?
2. How many miles up in space is the space shuttle expected to orbit?
3. Draw your own version of a space shuttle. Then use some construction paper to make a model of it.
4. What are meteoroids? How could a space shuttle be destroyed by them?
5. How is the space shuttle supposed to take off? How is it supposed to land?
6. How do manned flights differ from unmanned satellites?
7. What is meant by "light years?" Why can't man reach the nearest star system, Alpha Centauri, which is 43 light years away?
8. In as much detail as possible, explain what each of the following types of satellites is used for:

    communication   weather
    navigation   measuring magnetism
    surveillance   measuring gravitation

Other Books to Read about Space Shuttles
1. Bergaust, Erik. *Rescue in Space.* Putnam's, 1974.
2. Bergaust, Erik. *Space Stations.* Putnam's, 1962.
3. Branley, Franklyn. *Experiments in the Principles of Space Travel.* Crowell, 1973.
4. Coombs, Charles. *Skylab.* Morrow, 1972.
5. Rosenfeld, Sam. *Ask Me a Question about Rockets, Satellites and Space Stations.* Harvey, 1971.